A HISTORY OF GUN CONTROL

By. N. T. Gore

Copyright & Legal Notice

"Scales of Justice" – Museum San Diego / Pub. Dom.

Table of Contents

Introduction

"Guns are not the issue. We are." —
Aaron B. Powell

Since the horrible events that unfolded at Sandy Hook Elementary school in Newton Connecticut on December 14, 2012, the issue of gun control has been under the spotlight of the national headlines.

Gun control advocates and their antigun control counter parts have both been engaging in fear tactics and shady statistics in the press as a way to sway public opinion to their cause. It is easy to look at this issue through the lens of United States politics, as a liberal versus conservative issue. The reality cuts much deeper than that, of course. It doesn't take a lot of looking to find persons that having voted democrat in every election in their life are opposed to stricter gun control measures, and similarly, staunch republicans that would support the outright ban of privately owned fire arms can be found.

A reader's story:

"I was, maybe, twelve years old the first time that I remember the idea of gun control coming up. I had gone to visit my father, Albert, on his property in rural Skagit County, Washington. He had twenty acres on a hillside, and as we often did when I went to visit my father we went out to do some target practicing on the firing range he had constructed down by the creek.

While we were shooting our .22 caliber rifles at some soda cans set up on a hay bale at the far end of the range that day, he said to me, "Well, you know the government is planning on making everybody register their firearms? That's just the first step in them taking our guns away."

At the time I didn't understand what he was saying but once I was old enough to form my own opinion as an adult, I disagreed with him. Thinking back, that conversation with my father was the first time that I was exposed to other ideas about owning and using firearms.

Although my father's prediction has not come to pass, it weighed heavily on my mind over the nearly thirty years since we had that conversation. Whenever the issue of gun control rears its head in the news; I think back upon that day."

For all its current trendiness, the issue of gun control is not a new one, however. From almost the instant that the first firearms were invented there have been efforts to control their ownership.

The issue of gun ownership and usage rights has been with us for some 800 years now, and it is not going away anytime soon. Gun control is an issue for our time, but more than that it is an issue for all times and places that firearms exist.

But what is the history behind it?

What This Book Will Do

When delving into the history of a subject it is helpful to define exactly what that subject consists of, so that the author or compiler of said history and the readers are on the same page, so to speak. In this book, gun control will be defined as 'any attempt by person or persons in positions of authority to limit the ownership or use of fire arms by private citizens'.

This includes attempts by governments and governmental agencies at all levels, global, national and more localized. Technically, larger international bodies such as the United Nations should be included as well, but for space reasons this book will not consider them.

Basically, this book will attempt to chronicle the saga of those in power attempting to limit the access of firearms to those who are not in power.

Of course such an undertaking, if attempted in exhaustive detail would take much more space than this one book will permit, so what we will be presenting here is a short overview of gun control from pre-modern times to the present and tomorrow, followed by a section dealing with specific examples of gun control measures in various places around the world in the 20th century.

Finally, we conclude this book with a more in-depth look at the history of gun control in the United States from the ratification of the Constitution until the present day - although some examples of state and local gun control measure will be looked at, this work will mostly focus on national gun control issues in the interest of saving space.

What This Book Will Not Do

In any piece of writing about the subject of gun control, one is tempted to take sides in the currently raging debate, and support the arguments of one side or the other.

This book will not do that, instead it will attempt to remain largely neutral in regards to the debate about whether stricter gun control laws are needed in the United States, or anywhere else in the world.

That is not to say that the debate will not be mentioned at times in the text, arguers from both sides often point to the past to support their arguments, often inaccurately. This book will attempt to set straight the record in such instances. Fear mongering rhetoric and inaccurate portrayals of historical fact do neither side of the debate justice.

It is neither this author's place nor inclination to try to convince the reader to support one side or the other of the gun control debate. It goes without saying that I do have an opinion on the issue, as do most people. I will be endeavoring to make sure that my opinion does not color the visor that history will be viewed through in this book, however.

In the end it will be up to you, the reader, to decide whether I have succeeded in this task.

Pre-Modern Gun Control

"Arms are the only true badge of liberty. The possession of arms is the distinction of a free man from a slave." — Andrew Fletcher

THE FOUNDATION OF MODERN U. S. GUN CONTROL

Much of the debate about the Second Amendment in the United States today rests its arguments in the historical common law of England, and because of that a look at gun control in England and its colonies in the time before the American Revolution is vital for anybody hoping to understand the issues.

While the 'right to bear arms' has long been a staple of English common law, and is codified in the Magna Carta and other early legal documents detailing individual rights, England has a long history of restricting firearm usage.

These restrictions started early on in England's history, once firearms became available, and extend to the present day.

The early gun laws of England often restricted both certain types of fire arms, such as wheel locks which were outlawed during the reigns of King Henry VII and King Henry VIII, and who exactly could own and use firearms.

Other restrictions appear to be targeted at keeping guns away from the reach of the poor majority, and in the hands of the social elite and government controlled military. During the year 1541 King Henry VIII decided to limit the lengths of firearms that citizens could possess[1].

Longer guns could still be kept in the home for defensive purposes, but not carried in public, and guns could not be fired within a quarter mile of a town unless it was for defense of self or home, or at a shooting range. That same year Parliament moved to restrict gun ownership to the nobility and rich land owners.

After the revolution, the restored monarchy even took an interest in monitoring the distribution of guns. Constance Emerson Crooker says that "in 1660, Charles II tracked the sale of firearms by requiring gun makers to report all gun sales including the person to whom the guns were sold, and to list all guns held in stock,"[2]

And in 1671, he amended the Hunting Act to restrict hunting to wealthier land owners and declared persons unable to meet this requirement "to be persons by the laws of this realm, not allowed to have or keep for themselves, or any other person or persons, any guns, bows, greyhounds...."[3] allowing the government to disarm the preponderance of the kingdom who were not among the wealthiest of land owners.

Of course, there was always back and forth play between a monarch and his realm in such matters and David T. Hardy says that "As Charles' reign wore on he encountered increasing opposition from Parliament."[4]

While the English monarchs might have wanted to keep guns under control, free thinkers and politicians often held differing beliefs. Andrew Fletcher, the great Scottish statesman quoted at the beginning of this section, was a huge proponent of the right to bear arms, and political philosopher John Locke wrote of the right to bear arms as basic to human existence in his Second Treatise on Government.

EARLY GUN CONTROL AND RELIGION

Religion, as can be expected, also played a major role in the right to own guns. When a Catholic monarch came to the throne all Protestants were duly disarmed, and when a Protestant monarch was crowned the Catholics were similarly disarmed while the Protestants found their 'rights' restored.

This was common practice not only in England, but elsewhere in Europe as well, wherever conflict between Catholics and Protestants existed.

In the Holy Roman Empire, the treaties of Augsburg in 1555 and Westphalia in the 1640s both affirmed that the 'prince' or ruler of a province or territory had the right to name the official brand of Christianity in that territory, and common practice when doing so was to disarm those that observed other denominations to prevent uprisings. No matter what sort of Christianity the ruler supported, it was often understood that Jews and other non-Christians would be restricted from owning firearms.

Although it would not reach its crescendo until the late 1930s and the early 1940s in Germany, the persecution of those of Jewish faith had a long history in Europe. When the infamous Spanish inquisition began it was looking not for witches, but for *conversos* (Jews that had converted to Christianity) that had slipped back into Jewish practices.

Pogroms can be much more easily carried out if the targets that are being persecuted are not allowed to own weapons, and pre-modern Europeans understood this just as well as modern people do.

This is not to say that Jews and Muslims living with in Europe were prevented from owning arms in all times and place; but the denial of arms to such as them was the rule rather than the exception for much of European history.

HOW GUN CONTROL SPARKED THE AMERICAN REVOLUTION

When the 'shot heard round the world' was fired on April 19 1775 in Massachusetts, it was in response to a troop of British soldiers on their way to disarm the people of Lexington and Concord.

Some 700 British soldiers had orders to capture militia supplies, mainly consisting of firearms, which were being stored in Concord. Little did the British realize that the colonials had ascertained weeks beforehand that such a strike might be coming, relocating most of the supplies in question well before the British left Boston.

The American colonists had always been more gun friendly than their kin across the sea in England, they had after all, needed firearms to tame the wilderness of a vast new continent. Not only had the early colonists brought their own firearms with them, but the government also supplied them with extra guns, shot and powder, and this can be seen as the beginning of the so called 'gun culture' in America, it has been with us far longer than most imagine.

While not the only factor leading to the revolution, British attempts to disarm American colonists played a major role in the buildup to the revolution, and the attempt to capture the Concord militia supplies was the spark that set off the powder keg that had been building up pressure for some time.

---

[1] Henderson, <u>Gun Control</u>, pp. 86
[2] Crooker, <u>Gun Control and Gun Rights</u>, pp. 45
[3] 22 & 23 Car. II, c.25 (1671).
[4] Hardy, "The Right To Keep and Bear Arms," par. 17

World Gun Control In The 20ᵗʰ Century

> *"Every good communist should know
> that political power grows out of the
> barrel of a gun." — Mao Tse-tung*

EUROPEAN ATTITUDES TOWARD GUN
CONTROL

Gun Control, as a subject, is much more popular
among the people of Europe than it is with American
citizens. This section is an over view of Europe as a whole,
and it should be understood that not everything in this
section applies toward every nation within Europe.

Many European countries have what many
Americans would consider undue restrictions on firearm
possession and ownership. However, there are many
differences between the types of gun control laws that are
most common in Europe and what the average American
thinks of as 'gun control.'.

Don Kates says "…European gun laws are often
different from ours. This is largely because they aim to
stem political violence, not apolitical gun crime. But they
are not generally more restrictive."[1]

The following is very important to note. While more
registration and licensing may be required by the typical
European, when he or she goes about actually using those
guns the shooter often is more legally safe than a
counterpart in the United States is.

In Germany, shooting a man stealing from your apple orchard is perfectly justified under the law, and in Italy, France, Germany or Austria a woman can be justified in shooting an attempted rapist even if he breaks off the attack and tries to flee, a situation that would lead to assault or manslaughter charges should it happen in the United States.[2]

Oftentimes, certain styles or calibers of weapons are highly restricted in European nations.

9mm handguns, one of the most popular calibers in America, are often available only be special permit which is rarely given out, certain calibers of rifles are also restricted in this same way.

This can lead Americans looking at it from afar to conclude that the nation in question has draconian regulations on fire arm ownership, when in fact this often not the case.

The 9mm handgun and rifle calibers that are restricted are often what the government considers 'military grade', and other calibers of handgun and rifle often have little or even no restrictions on their purchasing and possession.[3]

Modern British Gun Control

Modern Britain has gun control regulations that are very strict from the point of view of the typical American, in fact, they are some of the strictest gun control measures in Europe. The British have always been more accepting of gun control, it seems, and the current draconian level of gun control enjoys wide spread popular support in Britain.

The British gun control laws got ever stricter over the course of the 20th century until they arrived at their current form around 1997.

The Pistols Act of 1903 was the first modern British law to place restrictions on the sale of fire arms, specifically pistols.

The Pistols Act made it illegal to rent or sell a pistol to anybody without a current game or gun license, although certain exceptions applied. The Pistols Act had limited effectiveness, however, because anybody wishing to buy a pistol could simply purchase a license at any post office.

The Firearms Act of 1920, partly a least a response to rising numbers of firearms becoming available in the aftermath of World War One, had more teeth. The Act amended the law relating to firearms and other weapons and ammunition and was also meant to enable the government to control the overseas arms trade.[4]

The Firearms Act made it mandatory for anybody that wanted to buy or possess a firearm to have a firearm certificate, and ammunition was similarly limited. Such firearms certificates were very specific, each one detailing what gun or guns and how much ammunition a person could possess.

Acquiring a firearms certificate could be more difficult than a gun or game license had been under the older laws, as well; they were given out by the local chief constable who had the power to exclude people for any number of reasons, some of them extremely vague in wording.

The Firearms Act of 1937 incorporated various changes to the Act of 1920, and expanded it to include smoothbore firearms, such as shotguns, which had not been covered by the 1920 Act. The act of granting certificates for machine guns was transferred to the military's discretion, such certificates were rarely granted and thus ownership of such weapons became extremely limited, restricted mainly to museums, police forces and the military itself.

The same year, in 1937, a ruling by the Home Secretary declared that 'self-defense' was no longer an acceptable excuse to apply for a firearms certificate, and chief constables around the nation were told to reject applications that came before them using self-defense as the sole justification.

The Firearms Act of 1968 introduced more controls on shotguns, and prohibited criminals that had served time in prison from owning firearms. This later restriction could range from a period of five years to a life time ban, depending on how long the criminal had been imprisoned for, and could be removed for an individual if they filed an application and had reasonable cause.

In the Wake of the 'Hungerford Massacre' in August of 1987, where gunman Michael Ryan killed sixteen people, wounded 15 others and then shot himself, the Firearms Amendment Act of 1988 was passed.

This act placed further restrictions of certain types of rifles and shotguns, and moved several more types of firearms to the restricted list, requiring military discretion as to who could purchase and possess them.

Nine years later, the Firearms Amendment No. 2 Act was passed in 1997, again in the wake of a tragic mass shooting. The Dunblane Massacre that spawned the Firearms Amendment No. 2 Act was reminiscent of the more recent Sandy Hook school shooting in the United States. On the 13th of March 1996, Thomas Hamilton entered the Dunblane Primary School and killed sixteen school children and one adult before killing himself with a self-inflicted gunshot wound to the head.

This tragedy rocked the United Kingdom, and the Firearms Amendment No. 2 Act quickly gained enough traction to pass. The Act almost completely banned the private possession of handguns, with some exceptions being made for black powder weapons, starter pistols, pest control pistols that fire shot cartridges, and pistols of special interest (either historical or esthetic).

This is very nearly the current state of gun control in Britain, a few other acts have passed since 1997, but rather than add more restrictions to firearm purchasing and possession they tend to focus on increasing the punishment for those that are caught using a firearm for a criminal purpose.

The Violent Crime Reduction Act of 2006 is an example of this type of legislation.

The question as to whether Britain's gun control measures have been successful or not is open for debate.

It is true that they have a much lower percentage of gun committed homicides by population than the United States does, but when violent crimes are looked at as a whole "the United Kingdom now leads the United States by an almost two-to-one margin" according to John R. Lott.[5]

While the gap may have narrowed in the decade since Lott wrote those words, Kates' more recent article claims that England's "murder rate is the highest in Western Europe and English violent crime overall is much higher than in the U.S. England annually has over 45,000 violent crimes per 100,000 population while the US has 33,600."[6]

Gun Control In Nazi Germany

Godwin's law states that "as an online discussion grows longer, the probability of a comparison involving Nazis or Hitler approaches 1," and while aimed at online discussions the same can be said of virtually any discussion in U. S. politics, and gun control is no exception.

Within days of the Sandy Hook tragedy, as politicians and the media were asking for something to be done about the 'epidemic of gun violence in America,' memes began filtering through various social media mediums, showing images of Adolf Hitler and warning us of the consequences of draconic gun control.

Who can't suppress a flinch, however slight, when they see a picture of Hitler, hand lifted in a Nazi salute, next to the words "everybody in favor of gun control raise your right hand."

This is not, of course, the first time that Hitler has been linked to overbearing gun control. Those who oppose stricter gun control laws resort to scare tactics just as often as those advocate for it, and there is no larger boogey man looming in western history that Adolph Hitler.

Organizations such as the Jews for the Preservation of Firearms Ownership (JPFO) have long been on the Nazi gun control bandwagon. Unfortunately for those attempting to make the comparison of stricter gun regulations harkening back to Nazi Germany, it is simply not true that

Hitler's regime introduced harsh gun control measures after he came to office.

Alex Seitz-Wald says "the Weimar Republic, the German government that immediately preceded Hitler's, actually had tougher gun laws than the Nazi regime."[7]

This is not surprising, after the defeat it endured in World War One, the German legislature accepted the terms of the Treaty of Versailles and passed a law "that effectively banned all private firearm possession, leading the government to confiscate guns already in circulation."[8]

By 1928, the Reichstag had begun to ease these regulations, but had introduced strict registration requirements still required separate licenses to own, sell, and carry firearms.

In point of fact, the 1938 law signed by Hitler that gun control detractors often cite actually did much the opposite of what they claim, deregulating the transfer and purchasing of shot guns, rifles, and ammunition.

At the same time, Seitz-Wald says "many more categories of people, including Nazi party members, were exempted from gun ownership regulations altogether, while the legal age of purchase was lowered from 20 to 18, and permit lengths were extended from one year to three years."[9]

Of course, gun control opponents often point out that the law also prohibited Jews and some other minorities from owning guns, and this is true. However, when looked at objectively, this becomes an issue of racism rather than gun control. The Nazis also placed a number of other restrictions on Jewish people, such as making Jews live in certain neighborhoods (ghettos), but we don't hear a hue and cry against the evils of urban planning. The JPFO and similar organizations often proclaim that had the Jews had the right to own guns in Nazi Germany the holocaust would have never happened.

This belief is naïve to say the least. After all, the Soviet Army with its artillery, tanks and planes lost over 7 million soldiers fighting the German war machine, is it really logical to assume that Jews with pistols, shotguns, and hunting rifles would have done better?

In the end, as Seitz-Wald says, "if guns don't kill people, then neither does gun control cause genocide (genocidal regimes cause genocide)."[10]

Soviet Gun Control

Before the Soviet Union existed, gun control in Tsarist Russia had been virtually non-existent.

Of course, this helped the Bolsheviks and other radical groups that were interested in changing the political landscape and they imported large number of firearms to outfit themselves for the revolution. Once they achieved a prominent position, the Bolsheviks attempted to disarm everybody else, generally with limited success.

When Joseph Stalin was collectivizing the peasantry, gun control once again reared its head. The spam emails and social media memes that claim 'In 1929, the Soviet Union established gun control. From 1929 to 1953, about 20 million dissidents, unable to defend themselves, were rounded up and exterminated,' are referring to this period of time.

Unfortunately for them, Stalin and the Soviet Union did not establish gun control in 1929; in fact, gun control laws had been established much earlier in the Soviet Union. What happened in 1929, is that when Stalin began the process of collectivization, the government began enforcing the laws as they stood in a much more aggressive manner.

This makes sense when one looks at the scope of what the government was trying to do, and the resistance it was meeting among the poor farmers and laborers that they were trying to do it to.

Nearly all of those rural farmers and laborers owned rifles as part of their livelihood derived from hunting. Stalin was just using good sense, if one plans on forcing a bunch of people to do something that they don't want to do, one should make sure that they have a hard time fighting back.

It should be noted that the second part of the meme's statement is very disingenuous as well, rather than being 'rounded up and exterminated,' most of the 20 million soviet citizens that died during that period starved to death during the famines caused by the abject failure of collectivization.

After Stalin's death, Soviet gun control efforts eased up a bit; although urban areas were still subject to strict regulation. Stalin's attempts to disarm the rural peasants were not completely successful in the end, and after he was gone the government relaxed restrictions on them.

Until the very end of the Soviet Union, the rural folk would be allowed to own hunting rifles.

Gun Control In The People's Republic Of China

The Chinese government has taken Chairman Mao's words to heart - "Every good communist should know that political power grows out of the barrel of a gun." And in order to limit the political power of those people in their nation that might not want to tow the communist party line, they have largely abolished private gun ownership.

Exceptions are made for hunters, who can apply for a hunting permit that will allow them to apply for another permit so that they may purchase and hold firearms for that purpose (isn't bureaucracy wonderful).

Other than hunters, the only people allowed to carry a firearm in The People's Republic of China are the military, law enforcement and security personnel.

Despite the often harsh punishments for those illegally found possessing and selling firearms in China, black market gunrunning remains a big business.

According to Zhu Zhe between June and September of 2006 official figures show "police confiscated about 178,000 illegal guns, 3,900 tons of explosives, 7.77 million detonators and 4.75 million bullets."[11]

This should come as little surprise, as the amount of money made from selling a single black market firearm can often exceed triple what an impoverished farmer could make in a year.[12]

Still, information such as this does little to instill confidence in the idea that China's harsh gun control measures have kept guns out of the hands of criminals.

As was the case in the Soviet Union, Mao Tse-tung's attempts at collectivization ended in famine and failure, with millions of people perishing as a result. These deaths had little to do with any sort of gun control policies that Moa established, however.

The truth of the matter is that China had strict gun control laws, introduced to it by the Dutch and the British, prior to the communist revolution, and the new communist government found that those laws already suited their needs very well.

Of course, a factor leaning in favor of gun control in China has always been the crippling poverty of the peasantry. Even today, most rural farmers cannot afford to buy a firearm if they wanted to, and the same has been true since well before the communists came to power.

---

[1] Kates, "Myths of European Gun Laws," par. 2
[2] Kates, "Myths of European Gun Laws," par. 6-8
[3] Kates, "Myths of European Gun Laws," par. 9
[4] Greenwood, Firearms Control: A Study of Armed Crime and Firearms Control in England and Wales, pp. 27-29
[5] Lott, The Bias Against Guns, pp.77
[6] Kates, "Myths of European Gun Laws," par. 22
[7] Seitz-Wald, "The Hitler Gun Control Lie," par. 6
[8] Seitz-Wald, "The Hitler Gun Control Lie," par. 6
[9] Seitz-Wald, "The Hitler Gun Control Lie," par. 7
[10] Seitz-Wald, "The Hitler Gun Control Lie," par. 7
[11] Zhe, "China reiterates stance on gun control" Par. 10
[12] Zhe, "China reiterates stance on gun control" Par. 16

Gun Control In The United States

"Americans have the right and advantage of being armed - unlike the citizens of other countries whose governments are afraid to trust the people with arms." — *James Madison*

THE FOUNDING FATHERS

The Constitution of the United States was drawn up at the Philadelphia Constitutional Convention in 1787 and sent to the states for ratification. A sufficient number of states ratified the constitution and it went into effect that same year, but the process was not without a great deal of debate.

The arguments generally came down to a disagreement between two camps, the Federalists that supported the idea of a strong central government and the anti-federalists who feared that centralized power could be a threat to their newly acquired liberty.

Crooker says "in 1789, Congress responded to the anti-federalists' concerns by proposing the first Ten Amendments to the Constitution. These amendments are called the Bill of Rights. While the body of the Constitution delineates the powers according to the three branches of government, the Bill of Rights describes the relationship of the newly formed government to its people. These 10 amendments were ratified by the states in 1791."[1]

The Second Amendment to the U. S. Constitution in its entirety reads "A well-regulated Militia, being necessary to the security of a free State, the right of the people to keep and bear Arms, shall not be infringed."

This imposing sentence is the foundation for all of the gun laws enacted by the federal government of the United States, and the largest reason why the federal government waited so long to get involved in gun control at all.

Today, scholars on both sides of the gun control issue love to debate exactly what was intended with the Second Amendment and how the sentence should best be read to derive that intention.

Gun control advocates look to the first part of the amendment, and grasping onto the word militia contend that the Second Amendment was never intended to protect the individual right to bear arms, while gun control opponents point to the second half of the sentence and contend that 'the right of the people to keep and bear Arms, shall not be infringed' is self-explanatory.

Of course, we are now far removed from the days when the Bill of Rights was ratified, and our attitudes and ideas might not mesh as well with those of the founding fathers as we would like to believe.

By looking back to time periods earlier than our own, to see what people thought of the Second Amendment in the past, we see that many of them thought that the amendment guaranteed their right to bear arms at a personal level.

Hardy tells us that in 1825 William Rawle, a close friend of George Washington, and a man that had been offered first crack at the job of Attorney General wrote "No clause in the Constitution could by any rule of construction be conceived to give to Congress a power to disarm the people."[2]

Congress itself seemed to clarify its feelings on the matter in 1792, when the second congress adopted the Militia Act, a bill that stayed on the books until 1903.

The Militia Act contained an individual mandate that men between the ages of 18 and 45 had to belong to a militia, and furthermore, as Adman Winkler says, "mandated every eligible man to purchase a military-style gun and ammunition for his service in the citizen militia. Such men had to report for frequent musters—where their guns would be inspected and, yes, registered on public rolls."[3]

The United States Supreme Court even appeared to accept that the second amendment guaranteed the individual's right to bear arms, in what can, perhaps, be described as the worst way possible, when in 1856 the Dred Scott v. Sanford case was decided.

Chief Justice Taney wrote for the majority "It would give to persons of the negro race, who were recognized (sic) as citizens in any one State of the Union, the right to… keep and carry arms wherever they went."

These views lead Hardy to conclude that "Thus, from the subsequent enactments of Congress, as well as the contemporaneous statements of the drafters and their associates, there can be little doubt that the drafters of the Second Amendment viewed that amendment as creating an individual right to keep and carry arms for purposes ranging from self-protection to hunting to acquisition of military skills."[4]

State Level Gun Control

While the federal government would wait over a hundred and thirty years before establishing any sort of national gun control laws, the individual states began enacting them much sooner, with lesser and greater degrees of success.

Nearly every state (44 out of 50) has a clause in its state constitution guaranteeing a citizen's right to bear arms, and when the states began passing laws against the carrying of conceal weapons or what types of firearms could legally be purchased they often found themselves being taken to court over whether or not such laws were constitutional.

The first major case about this issue didn't involve a firearm at all, but it was still important to the issue of gun control and the right to bear arms. *Bliss v Commonwealth*, Kentucky 1822 (12 Ky. [2 Litt.] 90, 1822) was an appeal of a case where the defendant had been convicted under a Kentucky concealed weapons law. The defendant's argument was that the law which forbid his sword-cane violated the state constitution which said that "the right of the citizens to bear arms in defense of themselves and the state, shall not be questioned."

When rendering its verdict the court determined that the state constitution was clear, and that later in the constitution it expressly declared that "everything in that article is excepted out of the general powers of government, and shall therefore remain inviolate; and that all laws contrary thereto, or contrary to the constitution, shall be void."

In accordance with their finding, the court declared the statute that Bliss had been convicted under unconstitutional. Henderson summarizes the impact of the case by saying "although not involving a firearm, this is one of the earliest state decisions relating to weapons laws and the most absolute and its insistence on a totally unfettered turn right to bear arms. Its precedent is not followed in most subsequent decisions, which find at least some arms regulations… to be compatible with the constitutional right to bear arms."[5]

Nunn v State, Georgia 1846 (1 Ga. 243, 1846); Georgia is one of the states that quickly adopted very strict gun control measures, and Hawkins H. Nunn fell afoul of that law when he was caught with a pistol in his possession.

After being indicted and convicted, Nunn appealed and the case made it all the way to the state Supreme Court. The court, in its ruling struck down a part of the Georgia law that prohibited carrying of weapons openly, but maintained those parts of the law which regarded concealed weapons.

The implications of the Georgia Supreme Court's ruling suggests that state and federal constitutions ensure an individual as well as a collective right to bear arms, but goes on to conclude that State and local authorities can pass laws banning concealed weapons as dangerous to the community, and can make other regulations so long as the right to self-defense is maintained.

Many of the court rulings on gun control that would come before state Supreme Courts in the future would follow the *Nunn v State* precedent.

When the United States Supreme Court became involved in a case that involved state mandated laws regulating fire arms, *United States v Cruikshank*, 1876 (92 U. S. 542, 1876), they basically washed their hands of the whole affair, and said that the second amendment of the U.S. Constitution applied only to the federal government. In regards to *United States v Cruikshank* Henderson says "the Supreme Court decided that the second amendment… was a restraint only to congress, not to states, localities or citizens."[6]

The Old West

The 'Wild West' as we know it is largely a myth created by nostalgia, Hollywood Westerns, and dime novels. That has not, however, stopped gun control opponents from portraying this period of time (from the end of the civil war until the turn of the twentieth century) in the American West as some sort of golden age for gun ownership and carrying rights. The reality, as is often the case, was somewhat different, however.

The place is Tombstone Arizona, the date is October 26, 1881, and the time is 3:00 pm.

Four men, three armed with pistols and one with a shotgun tucked under his long coat, walk up the dusty street. At a vacant lot a few doors down from the local corral; they met another group of armed men. The two groups exchanged words and then thirty seconds of hell erupted as nearly all parties involved fired multiple shots. This was the famous 'gunfight at the OK corral,' and the issue of gun control lurked at its root.

Tombstone had passed town ordinance #9, which prohibited firearms from being carried in public. The wilderness around tombstone was known to be dangerous, however, so the ordinance allowed for the bringing of firearms into town, as it was recognized that they were a necessary tool for survival when outside of the city limits.

After arriving in town, an armed man was expected to store his firearms at his earliest convenience, and most saloons, hotels and liveries were happy to hold guns for visitors.

The Clantons, Ike and Billy, along with Tom and Frank McLowery had not stowed their guns in a timely fashion, and what is more they had been making threats against the Earp brothers in the days leading up to the confrontation.

When Town marshal Virgil Earp and his brothers, deputy marshals Wyatt and Morgan Earp, along with temporarily deputized John 'Doc' Holliday, walked down the street to confront the armed men they were acting with the full authority of the law behind them.

Douglass Linder says "The Earps knew from reports they had received that Frank McLaury, and Ike and Billy Clanton, were in violation of this Ordinance. The confrontation that led to the gunfight grew out of Virgil Earp's determination to enforced Tombstone's law prohibiting the carrying of deadly weapons."[7]

In the latter part of the 19th century and first decades of the 20th, there were still no laws regulating guns at the national level. Instead states, counties, and cities all decided upon their own gun control measures, if any.

The ordinance that Tombstone passed to restrict the carrying of firearms in town was by no means unusual for the time, and many western communities such as Dodge City in Kansas had similar laws in the books at one time or another.

Adman Winkler writes that, in fact, "Frontier towns -
- places like Tombstone, Deadwood, and Dodge -- actually
had the most restrictive gun control laws in the nation."[8]

As in the years leading up to the civil war, states and
territories would sometime adopt laws that went too far,
and in doing so would find their Supreme Courts
deliberating on the issue of gun control.

The Supreme Court of Idaho found themselves in one
such deliberation in 1902, *In re Brickey* (8 Idaho 597,
1902). Back in 1889, the territorial legislature (Idaho would
become a state the next year) passed an act that prohibited
private persons from carrying deadly weapons within the
limits or confines of any city, town, or village. Carter says
that "in making its decision, the court examined both the
second amendment and the state's constitutional provision
granting the right to bear arms for self-defense."[9]

The court determined that the aforementioned act
contravened "the provisions of the second amendment to
the federal constitution and the provisions of section 11,
art. 1, of the constitution of Idaho" and declared it void,
they went on to say that "While it is undoubtedly within the
power of the legislature to prohibit the carrying of
concealed deadly weapons, and such regulation is a proper
exercise of police power, yet the legislature does not
possess the power to prohibit the carrying of firearms, as
the right to do so is guaranteed (sic) to the citizen both by
our federal and state constitutions."[10]

Depression Era Gun Control

The first federal legislation that could be termed considered 'gun control' showed up just before this nation was plunged into the great depression. The Miller Act of 1927, signed by President Coolidge on February 9, took effect on May 10 of that year.

The Miller Act made illegal the shipping of concealable handguns through the U. S. mail, although it did not prohibit the shipping of such weapons through private delivery companies such as the United Parcel Service.

The act got its name from John Miller, the republican congressman from the state of Washington that wrote it. The Miller act is still in effect, although the more sweeping gun control measures that were to come have eclipsed it.

While the Miller Act had little effect, since it was so easy to go around it by using other courier services, the next time the federal government would decide to get into gun control it would not leave so many loopholes.

1934's National Firearms Act (or NFA) mandated that seller and owners of such weapons as machine guns and sawed-off shotguns must register with the Collector of Internal Revenue and pay applicable taxes for firearm transfer.

The NFA is commonly seen as governmental response to the much publicized 'gangster' style violence that ran rampant in the early 1930s, with such outlaws as John Dillinger, Pretty Boy Floyd, and Bonnie and Clyde often outgunning the officers charged with their apprehension.

Therefore, the NFA targets the sorts of weapons that these types liked to use in their crimes.

Gregg Carter says that "the NFA was enacted under the taxing power granted to Congress in... the U.S. Constitution. It was administered by the secretary of the treasury, who has delegated all control to the Bureau of Alcohol, Tobacco, and Firearms (BATF)."[11]

The NFA applies only to fully automatic weapons and certain short-barreled long arms, it does not apply to handguns.

In addition to the applicable tax for transfer or sale of such a weapon - $200, which was not an insignificant sum back in 1934 - the NFA also requires that the permission of the BATF be granted before any such sales go forward, although back when the NFA was first put into effect local law enforcement often handled the granting, or not, of such permission.

The NFA is still in effect today, but it has been largely superseded by the Fire Arms Owners Protection Act of 1986, which made it illegal for private citizens to own or sell machine guns made after the year it was enacted.

Four years after the NFA was passed, the government would impose limitations on the sale of all firearms for the first time.

The Federal Firearms Act of 1938 "requires that manufacturers, importers and dealers in firearms (and ammunition for pistols and revolvers) obtain licenses" according to Henderson.[12]

The law also prohibits knowingly delivering a gun to a criminal or person under indictment, but as there are no requirements for any sort of background checks called out in the Federal Firearms Act, this part of the act proved unenforceable.

The Gun Control Act of 1968 repealed the Federal Firearms Act, but recycled many of the Federal Firearms Act's key components into itself.

Gun Control And Civil Rights

The issues of gun control and civil rights have long gone hand in hand, but not always in the way that one might think. It is true that the founding fathers didn't consider people of minority backgrounds to be 'citizens' with a right to bear arms.

Chief Justice Taney's statement in the Dred Scott case, implying the dangers of black citizenship and the rights that would grant, show little advancement in attitudes over the first fifty or so years of our nation's history.

Yet in the years after the civil war several laws were passed, not to keep guns out of the hands of blacks, but to ensure that they had the same right to bear arms as everybody else.

In 1866, the Freedman's Bureau Act, the Civil Rights Act, and the Fourteenth Amendment to the U. S. Constitution all include the second amendment right to bear arms as a right that a state is prohibited from taking away from any citizen.

These acts (and the fourteenth amendment) were at least partly in response to the 'black codes'. Adam Winkler states "After losing the Civil War, Southern states quickly adopted the Black Codes, laws designed to reestablish white supremacy by dictating what the freedmen could and couldn't do. One common provision barred blacks from possessing firearms."[13]

Of course, the convergence of gun control and civil rights has not always come at a time of minority need.

Winkler asserts that the Gun Control Act of 1968 was at least partially in response to 'fear inspired by black people with guns.'[14]

The Gun Control Act, which will be dealt with more fully below, was not without controversy; one of its provisions was in restricting the import of inexpensive, poor quality handguns of the type commonly referred to as 'Saturday night specials'.

Winkler comments, "Because these inexpensive pistols were popular in minority communities, one critic said the new federal gun legislation 'was passed not to control guns but to control blacks.'"[15]

That characterization of the bill is likely unfair, but Winkler's assertion that the "The gun-control laws of the late 1960s" were at least in part, "designed to restrict the use of guns by urban black leftist radicals,"[16] has some merit.

Modern American Gun Control Laws

The Federal Aviation Act (FAA), passed in 1958, had many different parts, but the section that is pertinent to this book prohibited the carrying of firearms by any passenger on or about a commercial flight.

Before the FAA , there were no regulations about taking firearms on airplanes. This section of the Federal Aviation Act was virtually the only federal gun control legislation passed in the thirty year period between the Federal Firearms Act in 1938, and the Gun Control Act of 1968.

The Gun Control Act (GCA) came at least partially as a response to the shooting deaths of such public figures as John and Robert Kennedy, Malcolm X, and Martin Luther King.

Like the NFA, the enforcement of the GCA is entrusted to the BATF. The GCA was primarily aimed at stopping interstate commerce of firearms, and put an end to interstate gun transfers except by licensed gun sellers and manufacturers.

The GCA also created a prohibited list, detailing what people gun sellers would not be allowed to sell firearms or ammunition to.

According to section 922 of the GCA, this includes: persons who have renounced their United States citizenship, any person who has ever been convicted of a crime that carries a sentence of over 1 year in prison, any person under indictment for such a crime, users of illegal drugs, any one that has been adjudicated as a mental defective or has been committed to any mental institution, illegal aliens, and anyone that has received a dishonorable discharge from the military; later additions to the act add anybody that has ever been convicted of a domestic violence charge (even if a misdemeanor) and those persons "subject to a court order that restrains such person from harassing, stalking, or threatening an intimate partner of such person or child of such intimate partner or person, or engaging in other conduct that would place an intimate partner in reasonable fear of bodily injury to the partner or child."

The GCA has been the basis for gun law in the United States since it was passed in 1968, with more recent acts modifying or adding to it.

Some examples of this are the Armed Career Criminal Act of 1984 which imposed fines and prison sentences for persons of the 'prohibited class' that were caught possessing or transporting a firearm as well as increasing the penalties for using a firearm in the commission of a felony, and the 1994 Violence against Women Act, which resulted in the addition of domestic violence offenders to the GCA prohibited list, as noted above.

Of course, the GCA is not without its detractors, particularly those who saw it primarily as a means to disarm young black militants, as was discussed previously.

Two acts were passed in 1986, the Law Enforcement Officers Protection Act, which outlawed the so called 'cop killer' bullets, ammunition that was designed to be able to penetrate body armor; and the Firearms Owners Protection Act, which relaxed some of the previous restriction to a certain extent but also introduced a near complete ban on fully automatic weapons made after the year it was adopted.

The Firearms Owners Protection Act supersedes the 1934 National Firearms Act, and the BATF will automatically reject applications related to the purchasing of fully automatic weapons created after 1986. Older automatic weapons still fall under the purview of the National Firearms Act, however, and requests for permission to purchase such weapon can still be made to the BATF along with the payment of the applicable tax, which is still set at $200.

1993s Brady Handgun Violence Prevention Act was named after former White House press secretary James Brady, who was crippled by a bullet from John Hinckley during Hinckley's assassination attempt of President Ronald Reagan.

The so called 'Brady Bill' required that persons wishing to purchase handguns must undergo a five day waiting period as a 'cooling off period' and to give dealers a chance to perform a background check. However, in 1998 the waiting period was eliminated in favor of an instant background check system.

It is important to note that the background check stipulation of the Brady Handgun Violence Prevention Act only applies to licensed gun dealers, Carter indicates, "at gun shows and flea markets in most states, guns can be bought and sold by unlicensed individuals. An estimated 4o percent of gun sales occur at gun shows, flea markets, among friends, and other 'unregulated' secondary markets."[17]

Whether the background checks make it more difficult for criminals to get guns is another question. Lott says that states that are 'open' or no background checks required at gun shows, criminals are 36 percent more likely to acquire their firearms in the state that they live in, rather than going traveling to another state to get their guns.

Of course, this statistic might not be as clear cut as it seems, because he continues on by saying that 'open states' have a much higher rate of gun ownership "indeed, the gun ownership rate in open states is 39 percent higher. To the extent that criminals obtain guns through theft those criminals living in closed... low gun ownership states are going to be much less successful on average in obtaining guns through theft."[18]

Efforts to pass legislation closing this alleged 'loophole' have ended in failure thus far.

Hailed as a great victory at the time by gun control advocates, the Assault Weapon Ban of 1994 banned the manufacture and sale of 19 different types of semi-automatic weapons that the government deemed to be 'assault weapons.'

Unfortunately for those that pushed the ban through, it did not have the marked influence of dropping crime rates that had been hoped for, and Congress allowed the Ban to expire in 2004.

In the aftermath of the Sandy Hook tragedy, where shooter Adam Lanza used a rifle that could be considered an assault weapon, there has been some talk about renewing the ban or crafting a similar piece of legislation, but such efforts appear to have stalled.

The 2005 Protection of Lawful Commerce in Arms Act was not so much a gun control initiative as it was a gun manufacturing protection initiative.

Carter states that "frustration with the lack of progress of the public health and law enforcement approaches to controlling gun violence has led many gun control advocates to place their hope in the judicial system—using it to sue gun manufacturers, wholesalers, retailers, and gun owners in civil court."[19]

The Protection of Lawful Commerce in Arms Act combats this practice by making manufacturers, dealers and distributers exempt from civil liability actions for any harm caused by the unlawful misuse of their products.

---

[1] Crooker, Gun Control and Gun Rights, pp. 46

[2] Hardy, "The Right To Keep and Bear Arms," par. 56

[3] Winkler, "The Secret History of Guns," par. 12

[4] Hardy, "The Right To Keep and Bear Arms," par. 58

[5] Henderson, Gun Control, pp. 41

[6] Henderson, Gun Control, pp. 47

[7] Linder, "Ordinances Enforced by the Earps in the OK Corral Shoot-out". Famous Trials: The O. K. Corral Trial.

[8] Winkler, "Did the Wild West Have More Gun Control Than We Do Today?" par. 2

[9] Carter, Gun Control in the United States: A Reference Handbook, pp. 198

[10] *In re Brickey* (8 Idaho 597, 1902)

[11] Carter, Gun Control in the United States: A Reference Handbook, pp. 156

[12] Henderson, Gun Control, pp. 92

[13] Winkler, "The Secret History of Guns," par. 35

[14] Winkler, "The Secret History of Guns," par. 30

[15] Winkler, "The Secret History of Guns," par. 33

[16] Winkler, "The Secret History of Guns," par. 40

[17] Carter, <u>Gun Control in the United States: A Reference Handbook</u>, pp. 162

[18] Lott, <u>The Bias Against Guns,</u> pp.202

[19] Carter, <u>Gun Control in the United States: A Reference Handbook</u>, pp. 98

American Federal Gun Control By Year

1789 – The Bill of Rights to the U.S. Constitution

1927 – The Miller Act

1934 – The National Firearms Act

1938 – The Federal Firearms Act

1958 – The Federal Aviation Act

1968 – The Gun Control Act

1984 – Armed Career Criminal Act

1986 – The Firearms Owner Protection Act

1986 – Law Enforcement Officers Protection Act

1988 – Terrorism Firearms Detection Act

1990 – The Crime Control Act

1993 – Brady Handgun Violence Prevention Act

1994 – The Gun Free Schools Act

1994 – Violence Against Women Act (VAWA)

1994 – The Assault Weapons Ban Bill

1996 – Domestic Violence Offender Gun Ban

2002 – Nonimmigrant Aliens Firearms and Ammunition Amendments

2005 – The Protection of Lawful Commerce in Arms Act

The Future Of Gun Control In The United States

"If we don't get gun-control laws in this country, we are full of beans. To have the National Rifle Association rule the United States is pathetic. And I agree with Mayor Michael Bloomberg: It's time to put up or shut up about gun control for both parties." - Harvey Weinstein

Cities with very strict local gun control ordinances, such as Chicago, continue to have very high levels of violent crime, while many rural areas with laxer regulations and higher rates of gun ownership tend to have very low amounts of violent crime.

However, it can be misleading to infer a direct cause-effect relationship between local gun control conditions and violent crime rate, as there are often other factors that are of equal or even greater importance to account for.

In the wrong hands, a gun can be used to create horrible tragedies, like the one at Sandy Hook Elementary School, but the onus for the tragedy is rightly placed on the person whose agency was responsible for the actions, rather than on the inanimate tool used to carry out the task.

The vast majority of gun owners in America are law abiding citizens. A criminal is not going to care if selling an AR15 assault rifle is legal or not, they undergo no background checks or waiting periods when buying a stolen pistol from the shady guy on the corner.

Bibliography And Further Reading

Carter, Gregg Lee, 2006. <u>Gun Control in the United States: A Reference Handbook</u>, Santa Barbra: ABC CLIO

Crooker, Constance Emerson, 2003. <u>Gun Control and Gun Rights</u>, Westport, CT: Greenwood Press

Croxton, Derek and Anuschka Tisher, 2002. <u>The Peace of Westphalia: A Historical Dictionary</u>, Westport, CT: Greenwood Press

Greenwood, Colin, 1972. <u>Firearms Control: A Study of Armed Crime and Firearms Control in England and Wales</u>, London: Routledge.

Henderson, Harry, 2000. <u>Gun Control</u>, New York: Facts On File Inc.

Hughes, Michael, 1992. <u>Early Modern Germany, 1477-1804</u>, Philadelphia: MacMillan Press and University of Pennsylvania Press

Kates, Don B., "Myths of European Gun Laws." 18 March 2013.
<http://www.calgunlaws.com/myths-of-european-gun-laws> (20 June 2013)

Linder, Douglass, 2005. Famous Trials: The O. K. Corral Trial,
<http://law2.umkc.edu/faculty/projects/ftrials/earp/earphome.html> (20 June 2013).

Lott, John R., 2003. The Bias Against Guns, Washington DC: Regnery

Nesbit, Lee ed., 2001. The Gun Control Debate: You Decide, Amherst: Prometheus Books

Seitz-Wald, Alex. "The Hitler Gun Control Lie." 11 January 2013. <http://www.salon.com/2013/01/11/stop_talking_about_hitler> (20 June 2013).

Stevens, Richard W., and Aaron Zelman, 2001 Death by "Gun Control": The Human Cost of Victim Disarmament, Hartford WI: Mazel Freedom Press

United States Senate, Report of the Senate Judiciary Committee Subcommittee on the Constitution, 97th Cong., 2d Sess., "The Right to Keep and Bear Arms," Committee Print I-IX, 1-23 (1982)

Winkler, Adam. "The Secret History of Guns." 24 July 2011. <http://www.theatlantic.com/magazine/archive/2011/09/the-secret-history-of-guns/308608/> (20 June 2013).

Winkler, Adam. "Did the Wild West Have More Gun Control Than We Do Today?" 9 September 2011. <http://www.huffingtonpost.com/adam-winkler/did-the-wild-west-have-mo_b_956035.html> (20, June 2013)

Zhe, Zhu, "China reiterates stance on gun control." 21 April 2007. <http://www.chinadaily.com.cn/china/2007-04/21/content_856308.htm> (20 June 2013)

Space For Reader's Notes

From the Author:

I hope you found this book interesting. Now that you have finished my book, please consider recommending it in a review. Reviews are the best way readers evaluate and discover great new books and I would truly appreciate it. You can post a review here:

www.amazon.com/author/ntgore

Thank you very much!

www.ingramcontent.com/pod-product-compliance
Lightning Source LLC
Chambersburg PA
CBHW021548200526
45163CB00016B/3024